UNBREAKABLE PATH

Unbreakable Path
A Story of Loss, Resilience, and the Pursuit of Greatness

Charlie Horky

©2025 All Rights Reserved. No portion of this book may be reproduced, stored in a retrieval system, or transmitted in any form or by any means—electronic, mechanical, photocopy, recording, scanning, or other—except for brief quotations in critical reviews or articles without the prior permission of the author.

Published by Game Changer Publishing
Cover Design: Skylar Ringenbach
Cover Photo: Heidi Gibbs

Paperback ISBN: 978-1-967424-37-5
Hardcover ISBN: 978-1-967424-38-2
Digital ISBN: 978-1-967424-39-9

www.GameChangerPublishing.com

Read This First

Just to say thanks for buying and reading my book,
I would like to connect with you!

Scan the QR Code Here:

Unbreakable Path

A Story of Loss, Resilience, and
the Pursuit of Greatness

CHARLIE HORKY

PROLOGUE
December 13, 2012

The pounding at the door came before dawn.

I heard Terrell shouting, then the sound of splintering wood as my front door was blown off its hinges. Seventy FBI agents in tactical gear swarmed into my Las Vegas ranch house, weapons drawn.

The timing couldn't have been worse. It was National Finals Rodeo week, and I had about fifty cowboys staying at my place, their horse trailers parked around the property. The agents herded everyone outside, lining them up by the barn in the cold desert morning. My security man stood helpless as our dogs ran wild, barking at the chaos.

I was placed in handcuffs, still in my underwear. "Charlie's not coming back anytime soon," the agents told my guests.

As I stood there watching my world implode, powerless to stop it, I couldn't help but appreciate the irony. Just twenty-four hours earlier, I'd been in a VIP room at the casino, rubbing shoulders with high rollers.

A few years before that, I'd owned the second-largest limousine company in America. I drove for Michael Jackson, Elizabeth Taylor, Quincy Jones, Sting, and Mick Jagger, among other celebrities. I'd handled transportation for the Royal Family of Brunei. I'd seen nearly $300 million pass through my hands.

Now, I was about to lose everything. Again.

The strangest part? This wasn't even my first time watching it all slip away.

But this time, things felt different. At fifty-two years old, I was running out of chances to start over. Or maybe because this time, unlike all the others, I had finally found something real to lose.

TABLE OF CONTENTS

BEGINNING – 1960s–1980s 1

RISE – 1987–1995 33

PEAK – 1995–2000 49

FALL – 2000–2012 67

REDEMPTION – (2012–Present) 91

BEGINNINGS
1960s-1980s

My name is Charlie Horky, and I've been told that my story would make a good movie. Maybe it would. But I think it might make a better cautionary tale: a story about how success without guidance can be as dangerous as failure and how sometimes you need to lose everything to find what matters in life.

I was born in Chicago to a family that straddled two worlds. My mother's side were Jewish immigrants from Russia, educated and cultured, who had made their fortune in the garment business. My uncle, Mo Morris, had developed something with recycled women's pantyhose that Eastman Kodak bought, sending him into the financial stratosphere. When he died in 1986, he was worth $50 million.

My father's side was different. They were Christian, old-school conservatives from Riverside. My great-grandmother owned a mortuary on Roosevelt Boulevard that had been in the family for 150 years. As a kid, I used to play with my sister in the casket room, not knowing what it was. My great-grandmother was friends with Al Capone—she even handled the burials after his St. Valentine's Day Massacre.

Both sides had their own definition of success. The Jewish side produced doctors and lawyers who played golf and took their place in society. My father went to Grinnell College and became a cardiologist. But he was also the one who would tear our family apart.

Visiting my aunt at age four — 1st birthday (Chicago, 1964).

When I was four, we moved to Los Angeles. That first move was brief, as we quickly relocated to Coronado, Colorado, where my father served two years in the military. I attended Miss Bunny's Day School, went to parades, and accompanied my mother to see The Beatles' *A Hard Day's Night*.

My parents were taken with the California lifestyle. After a brief return to Chicago, where some of my strongest memories were of all the presents I got in December (Christmas, Hanukkah, and my birthday, all in one month!), we moved back to L.A. As it turned out, the California sunshine was preferable to the Chicago wind and rain—that was the only thing my parents agreed on.

When I was seven years old, my sister three, and my mother pregnant with my younger brother, my father walked out. It wouldn't have been too bad if he'd still wanted to be a dad. But he didn't—not as much as I wanted him to be one.

Frankly, that was the beginning of the end for me.

I tried everything I could to get his attention. I performed badly in school, thinking if I was bad enough, he would have to come and get me. My teachers would tell me I could do better if I wanted to. But I didn't want to do better. I wanted my father.

There were scattered outings, moments of hope that always ended in disappointment. Once, when I was nine, Dad picked us up one night in our pajamas. We flew PSA Airlines to San Diego and spent Thanksgiving with him. Then, the following year, we cried ourselves to sleep when he never showed up to do it again.

The worst was in eleventh grade. I drove to his house in Palos Verdes with two friends, unannounced. He answered the door as if he were greeting strangers. When I tried to introduce my friends, he cut me off: "That's nice, it was good to see you, but I'm busy right now. I'll see you another time." And he slammed the door in our faces.

That was a long ride home.

Don't get me wrong. My childhood wasn't all trauma. I had loving grandparents on both sides, a roof over my head, and clothes on my back. We were solidly middle class in 1960s Los Angeles.

But I had nobody to teach me how to be a man. Without that guidance, I didn't have much sense of self.

* * *

Things improved when I started riding horses with the girls who lived down the street. We'd go to Griffith Park, and for the first time in my life, I found I was good at something. This gave me enough confidence that by my senior year of high school, I landed a job at the A Bar A Ranch in Wyoming. It was a famous place where wealthy people came to play cowboy on vacation, but for me, it was freedom.

When I returned home, there was a note on the door from my mom: if I wanted to live there, I had to go to school.

I imagine some kids would see that as a wake-up call. I certainly did—but probably not in the way my mother expected.

To me, it was as if someone had handed me a million dollars.

The freedom to turn heel and walk away from my childhood home—to be 100% on my own—was thrilling.

Within days, I had my first job at Jeff Frank Auto Leasing in Westwood. They paid me $300 a week to wash cars and gave me a car to take home at night. I found a room to rent from a UCLA professor for $125 a month. I was eighteen years old and well on my way.

That job introduced me to a different world. I learned more in my first month there than I had in all my years of school. The education started with something simple: a beautiful Stutz Bearcat owned by one of the company heads. It had mink floor mounts and a wooden wheel that gleamed like honey in the sunlight.

I'd never seen anything like it. While I was washing it one day, I realized this car was something more than a transport vehicle. This car was theater. It was a complete experience that communicated something about the personality of the owner, their values, how they wanted to be seen, how they lived, and how they wanted to live. Every detail mattered, from the spotless windows to the fresh leather smell to the way the chrome caught the light.

That car taught me that luxury isn't in the price tag. It's in the experience.

One of my co-workers at Jeff Frank was a girl named Lexi Raines. She was twenty-one: fully an adult woman, at least to me. She'd been with Led Zeppelin—part of the party scene on Sunset Boulevard. And to my surprise and delight, she took a liking to me.

One night, while preparing the limos, the crew was doing cocaine. They offered me a line, and I can't say I fought to refuse it. It was my first taste of that life. The drugs, the music, the feeling of being somebody—it was all amazing and, as it would turn out, addictive.

* * *

It soon became obvious to me that washing cars wasn't going to cut it forever. I took a job with the Bel Air Patrol, working security from 10 p.m. to 6 a.m. Most of the guys on patrol were frustrated cops who couldn't make the force, carrying AR-15s and playing soldier. I was just nineteen, patrolling Sunset Boulevard between the 405 Freeway and Beverly Glen, checking on subscribers' homes.

The job was usually mind-numbingly boring—turning lights on and off, leaving different colored cards to prove we'd done our rounds. But that changed the night I got the call about an alarm going off at Barbra Streisand's house.

Her house sat behind gates that probably cost more than most homes. The alarm was screaming into the night, echoing off the perfectly manicured hedges. Following protocol, I went to the back door and found it open. Drawing my weapon—something I'd only done in training—I moved through the house, calling out "Bel Air Patrol!" in what I hoped was an authoritative voice.

The house was like a museum—all pristine furniture and awards on the walls. Then I heard it: the distinct sound of a shower running in the master bathroom. Who breaks into a house and decides to take a shower?

I found him there, a naked man probably in his forties, standing in Barbra Streisand's marble shower like he owned the place. When I asked what he was doing there, he gave me the most matter-of-fact answer: "I'm here to see Barbra." Like this was a perfectly normal way to arrange a meeting with one of the world's biggest stars.

Now I had a situation on my hands: a fully nude intruder in Barbra Streisand's shower. They don't exactly cover this in security guard training. I had to walk him out of the house, dripping wet, make him put his clothes back on—which was about as awkward as you'd imagine—and wait for the LAPD to arrive.

The police found the whole thing hilarious. I had to fill out an incident report that probably read like a comedy sketch: "Subject apprehended in Ms. Streisand's shower."

Looking back, it was my first real brush with the weird world of celebrity, where the normal rules don't apply, and anything can happen at any time. I didn't really grasp it then, but that night was preparing me for a career where the unexpected would become routine.

* * *

Soon, I found myself driving past a Budget Rent-A-Car in Brentwood. Maybe it was fate, maybe it was luck, but I happened to roll in on my motorcycle when Morris Mirkin and Ruben Bird, the founders of Budget, were visiting that location.

I asked them for a job as a lot manager. They didn't have any open positions but suggested I talk to a guy named Marc Fogel, who owned a Budget location nearby at Third and La Cienega. They said he was a young guy with a young crew, and maybe he would hire me. Sure enough, I showed up and was hired on the spot because the founders had referred me. Marc was probably 24 to my 19, but he and his mother, Rhoda, had figured out something crucial about L.A.: people wanted more than just normal rental cars. They were pioneers, renting Mercedes-Benzes, Alfa Romeos, Ferraris, and Porsches to the entertainment industry.

Walking into that lot was like entering another world. Instead of AR-15s and security protocols, there were gleaming luxury cars and movie stars. Instead of watching for intruders, I was watching how the rich and famous moved through life. It was exactly what I needed: a complete change of direction, a chance to learn a different kind of service altogether.

I didn't know it then, but I had stumbled into my calling. The skills that had made me a good security guard—attention to detail, ability to read people, staying calm under pressure—would serve me well in this new world. But instead of preparing for the worst in people, I would be bringing out their best.

* * *

In that Budget Rent-A-Car on Third and La Cienega, Marc and Rhoda were renting—no, selling—California dreams. And man, did it work.

Rock stars would fly into L.A., and we'd have their chosen cars waiting at their hotels. Jimmy Buffett wanted a Mercedes convertible even though he always had a chauffeur-driven limousine in other cities like New York. He said the Mercedes convertible was the only proper way to drive down Pacific Coast Highway.

Dan Fogelberg also wanted a Mercedes convertible. These stars all had different personalities, and they wanted the cars to reflect how they saw themselves.

Just as instructive was watching the different ways they used the service. The rockers wanted freedom: They'd take the keys themselves and disappear down Sunset Boulevard. The studio executives wanted control: They'd have their assistants map out every minute of their day. The old money wanted discretion: They'd use back entrances and private gates. Each group taught me something different about service.

The real education happened late at night. Dan Fogelberg's tour manager, Charlie Fernandez, would call at four in the morning to pick Dan up from the Record Plant studio. I'd walk in to find him jamming with Jimmy Buffett, Linda Ronstadt, Don Henley, or J.D. Souther. Prince was recording down the hall. The air was thick with cigarette smoke and creativity, and you could feel the electricity of something special happening.

One night stands out in particular. I had driven Nancy Wilson of the band Heart to a recording studio. "These Dreams" was the first number-one hit the band ever had, and Nancy's sister Ann usually sang the lead. I was in the limo waiting for Nancy all night long. When she finally came out of the studio, she said she had just recorded herself singing "These Dreams" for the first time. She wanted to play it for me, so I popped the cassette in and listened to Nancy sing that beautiful song as I drove her home.

Marc and Rhoda Fogel had given me a front-row seat to a world I'd only dreamed about, an education you couldn't get in any school. I was learning how to read people, how to anticipate their needs, how to turn service into an art form.

My father had walked out, but these rock stars were there now. And, honestly, they were teaching me about life. They showed me that success wasn't about following the path others had laid out but about creating your own. Each one of them had broken the rules to make it, and in their own way, they were teaching me to do the same.

That's not to say that breaking the rules always turned up roses for me. I managed to get myself in plenty of hot water. One night, after dropping my girlfriend Rachel off at the top of Beverly Glen, I fell asleep at the wheel and drove through someone's front porch. The balcony collapsed. It looked like a bomb had gone off. I managed to limp the shredded car back to the lot. I had just totaled a brand new Mercedes-Benz, and when I called Marc to confess, all he said was, "Okay, babe, just take one of the Datsun B210s home then."

I scraped my way out of that one, but my luck ran out when I later crashed my own Pontiac Trans-Am on the same road. Rather than face a DUI, I left my license in the car and ran to

Rachel's house. That dumb decision turned it into a hit-and-run charge—my first real brush with the law.

Marc, who owned the car, connected me with a criminal defense lawyer named Michael Yamaki, who would become a lifelong friend and savior more than once. By some miracle, he got my case dismissed. I dodged jail time. But that was the end of my time at Budget Rent-a-Car.

* * *

It was during this time that Eli Katzman, an Orthodox Jewish businessman who frequented Budget, asked if I wanted to go into business together. We'd struck up a friendship, and in fact, I—as only a half-Jew—acted as his *Shabbas Goy*, turning up at his house on Fridays to switch off his lights and otherwise handle the electricity.

One day he asked me, "Is there anything you think you could do?"

"Let's start a limo company," I said.

"Why a limo company?"

"I worked at one last year. I washed the cars and watched what they did. I grew up in L.A. I know where I'm going. It can't be that hard: pick people up, take them where they're going, take them home."

That was my entire business plan.

Our first limousine, a 1979 Cadillac formal, cost us $11,000. It was elegant and understated, the kind of car that whispered money rather than shouted it. Eli gave me a shot at 49% of the company if I could make something of it.

I was learning fast about service—how to make people feel special. But I can see now that something crucial was missing in my education. While I was getting a master class in handling rock stars, I was getting no education at all in handling money, contracts, or business relationships.

The Fogels ran their business like a well-oiled machine. They understood cash flow, credit lines, and fleet management: all the boring but essential stuff that keeps a business alive.

I wasn't interested in any of that. I was focused on the flash: the beautiful cars, the famous clients, the feeling of being somebody.

When Eli asked me about going into business together, I didn't even think to ask about the structure of our partnership, how we'd handle expenses, or what would happen if things went wrong. My entire business plan consisted of eleven words: "Pick people up, take them where they're going, take them home."

I had no idea how naive that was.

Looking back, I can see how my father's absence shaped this blind spot. I'd never had anyone teach me about money, future planning, or protecting myself in business relationships. I was hungry for approval, eager to please, and completely unequipped to handle the business side of success.

It was a combination that would come back to haunt me again and again.

Making the "Front Page" at age 21.

* * *

My first job was driving Bob Keeshan, aka Captain Kangaroo. I was so confident I knew what he looked like, I didn't bother bringing a sign to the airport. Of course, I missed him completely. Captain Kangaroo was a character he played in makeup and costume—Bob Keeshan looked nothing like that in real life! There was an important lesson there: always be prepared and never assume anything.

My introduction to Quincy Jones came through an aging driver named Dave Smith, who owned Sterling Coach. Dave was on his last leg in the business, but he had a roster of loyal clients, including Bob Newhart, Quincy Jones, Loretta Swit, David Soul, and Linda Carter. One by one, he started having me drive these people. I didn't understand then that he was setting me up for succession in the industry. I was just grateful for the work.

My first real lesson in handling high-level clients came one cold night at the Hollywood Bowl. I was driving Quincy and his wife, Peggy Lipton, who was a famous actress from *The Mod Squad*. During the show, I noticed she'd left her mink coat in the back of the car. The temperature had dropped, and I knew she'd want it. Most drivers would have waited in the car—after all, that was the job. But I grabbed the coat and went looking for them inside the venue.

Back then, security wasn't what it is today. I managed to find their box and deliver the coat. It seemed like a small thing to me.

But on the ride home, Quincy said something that would change everything:

"I know you don't work for Dave. I want your phone number."

I hesitated. In our business, taking another company's client—jumping lines, we called it—was taboo. "Mr. Jones, I can't do that," I said. "That's not how this works."

He looked at me for a long moment. "Charlie, if you need me to call Dave, I will. Otherwise, if you would take care of it and let him know that we're going to be using you from now on, I'd appreciate that."

The old me would have jumped at the opportunity without thinking about the consequences. But I'd learned enough by then to understand the importance of handling these transitions professionally.

I went to tell Dave in person—only to discover he'd been murdered in his motel room.

Divine intervention, maybe?

Regardless, it meant I could take on Quincy's business with a clear conscience. That relationship opened doors I never knew existed.

* * *

Behind one of those doors? None other than Michael Jackson.

I was introduced to Michael through Quincy. One day in 1982, Quincy called and asked me to come to the studio because he was making a record with Michael Jackson. That record was *Thriller,* which ended up selling an estimated 70 million copies. I spent months with them during the recording, watching, and learning. While working for Quincy, I got to see how the biggest names in the business operated behind the scenes.

Michael took a liking to me. "Let me see your car," he said one day. We went out to the back of the studio, where I had this big white stretch limousine. Michael wanted to go for a ride, so we cruised down Melrose. He wanted to window shop, but being Michael Jackson, even in those early days, meant drawing a crowd. When the restaurants started emptying out and people began chasing him, he took off running.

I had to whip the stretch around in the middle of Melrose, pull up alongside him, and shout, "Michael, Michael, now's a good time! Jump in!" He leapt into the back seat with that famous laugh of his. "Oh, that was so much fun," he said. "Let's do it again!" I had to explain that getting chased by crowds wasn't exactly part of our normal service package.

What really struck me about Quincy was how he treated everyone the same—whether you were Michael Jackson or the guy parking cars. He taught me that real power is about making people feel valued—not making people feel small. Years later, when I had my own company and was handling transportation for some of the biggest names in entertainment, I would think back to those early days with Quincy. He showed me that success in this business isn't just about providing a service—it's about building trust. You could have the nicest cars and the best drivers, but without trust, you had nothing.

Again, take Michael Jackson. When I started driving him, I was so worried about pleasing him. So I watched and I learned. Michael could have had any driver or car he wanted, but what he really valued—what I was able to give him—was someone who could create a bubble of normalcy in his decidedly un-normal life. Once I understood that, everything else fell into place.

* * *

Shortly after meeting Quincy Jones, I met Irving Azoff when I used to deliver cars to him from Budget Rent-A-Car. When I bought my first limousine, I mentioned it to a woman I had met at Irving's company. She knew Dan Fogelberg and told me that he didn't like his limo company. That's how he became one of my first clients in 1981, along with Quincy. I met The Police through a travel agent and picked them up as clients, too.

That's when I truly understood the power of having the talent on your side.

Typically, the tour manager would call the promoter and ask for a car. But I was tired of being at the promoters' mercy. Driven by a conviction that the business that was being kept from me simply ought to have been mine, I started playing things a little off-book.

The truth was, I had met Dan Fogelberg through Nina at Irving's company, Frontline Management. I met The Police around the same time through a travel agent who gave me the band very early on, in 1981.

Concert promoters typically provided transportation for the act. The tour manager would simply call the promoter and tell him his requirements, and the promoter would send the company he had contracted—which, almost all the time, was not me.

Dan Fogelberg wanted me. The Police wanted me. They would tell the promoters exactly who they preferred. But Rex King couldn't give a toss, as long as he didn't have to pay for it—so he went with the promoter's choice.

This was part of my education in how the industry worked. That's when I decided to take matters into my own hands and try to flip the table on the promoter.

It worked.

When Robert Plant was coming to play the Forum, his tour manager, Rex King, told me they were using the car service preferred by the promoter, Avalon Attractions. But I went to the airport anyway. Then I called the other company, pretending to be Rex, and sent them to the wrong terminal. When Plant's plane landed, I was the only car there.

"Charlie, I thought I told you we're using another company," Rex said.

"I was just dropping off Rod Stewart and saw your plane. Thought I'd say hi."

"Where's our car?" he said.

"No idea."

He got on his phone, ripped the heads off the Avalon Attractions people, and handed the account to me.

That ruse worked out for me, so I played it again with Van Halen. And again with Motley Crue. Finally, the Avalon people started to catch on, and their president, Brian Murphy, decided to test me. He gave me thirty minutes to get him from Sherman Oaks to an Eric Clapton show in Irvine—an impossible task in L.A. traffic.

As Brian tore into me from the backseat, I called a friend who owned a helicopter company. "Any chance you've got a helicopter on the Transamerica building downtown?" I asked, trying to block out the screaming from back.

He did. Eight hundred dollars to fly Brian to the show. I didn't know how I'd pay for it, but I knew this was my shot.

When I pulled up to the Transamerica building, Brian couldn't believe it. "There better be a helicopter on that roof," he warned. And there was.

I was still there later that evening when the helicopter brought him back. He walked right up to me and said, "Avalon Attractions is all yours." That meant every single concert venue, stadium, or racetrack in Southern California from Los Angeles down to San Diego that Avalon promoted was given to me, including the Ice Capades and the circus. From that day forward, every rock and roll band that played an Avalon venue—from the Universal Amphitheater to the Coliseum to the L.A. Sports Arena—was mine.

* * *

Keeping my nerve and standing up to the money was one important lesson. But you're in a business that requires you to resort to ordering a helicopter to win over a client, that teaches you other things, too. I was beginning to understand that the real opportunity wasn't in solving problems clients brought to you. It was in solving problems they didn't even know they had.

My business became about creating an experience so seamless, so perfect, that clients couldn't imagine using anyone else. Years later, when I had hundreds of cars and was handling transportation for some of the biggest names in entertainment, the fundamentals hadn't changed.

* * *

While I was learning the fundamentals of luxury service, I still hadn't grasped one of the most important lessons in this business: understanding power. I thought I knew who held the real power in Hollywood: the studio heads, the producers, the money people. But it took Victoria Principal to show me how wrong I was.

I got the job through Frank Moore, the father of my girlfriend at the time, who owned Coast Productions. They were shooting a Jhirmack shampoo commercial with Victoria, who at the time was riding high as a star of *Dallas*. I decided to put all my service lessons into practice: fresh coffee and tea in a thermos, a flower in the car, arriving early.

The morning was cool and misty when I pulled up to Victoria's house. In this business, you learn to read people in the first ten seconds—it tells you everything about how the day will go. Victoria stepped out and did something that surprised me: she introduced herself. "Hi, I'm Victoria," she said simply, as if I might not know who she was. No pretense, no attitude, just direct and professional. I introduced myself, and we headed to the shoot.

At the location, a production manager swaggered over to my window. "We won't need you until 7 p.m. when filming wraps," he said dismissively. This meant I'd get my two-hour minimum, about $112 for the day. Not much, but that's how it seemed to work.

Before leaving, I thought I should let Victoria know that I would see her later. I found her in her trailer, getting her hair done. When I explained I was leaving, she stopped everything. "Why are you leaving?" she asked, her tone shifting. When I told her what the production manager had said, she stood up, still in her robe with curlers in her hair, and took my hand. She walked me out to the set and said, "Please show me who said that."

When I pointed out the manager, she walked right up to him in front of the entire crew and said, "This is my driver, Charlie. And he's going to stay here the entire day, every day. You're going to pay for it. You're going to make sure he's comfortable, has a place to sit, and gets to eat. Do you understand me? Because if he's leaving right now, I'm leaving right now."

Victoria Principal

The three-day job ended up bringing in almost $2,000. But the real value wasn't in the money—it was in the lesson. Power flows from the top down, not the bottom up. Yes, you can work your way up from the bottom, but it's a much harder road. From that moment on, I understood that having the star's support was worth more than any connection with middle management.

Victoria later taught me another lesson about professional discretion. When she started dating Dr. Harry Glassman, she took me aside one day. "Listen, Charlie," she said, "when he's around, I need you to defer to him. It's his show when we're together." I appreciated her directness, and that instruction served me well throughout my career.

That shoot changed my entire approach to building my business. I started focusing on cultivating relationships with the real decision-makers, the ones who could make things happen. In Hollywood, power isn't always where you think it is. Sometimes, it's not in the corner office. It's in the trailer, sitting under a hair dryer, ready to go to bat for the right person.

* * *

In 1984, I had got out of my first partnership with Eli and found a new partner: none other than Irving Azoff, Dan

Fogelberg's manager and the president of MCA records. He wasn't a partner, exactly. In fact, when we incorporated the new business in 1984, he listed his wife Shelli as my co-owner.

Irving wasn't particular about the business's name. We just ended up calling it Charlie's Limousine Service. Later, I changed it to CLS.

He was also ambitious on my behalf. "One car?" he exclaimed. "You have lots of people you're driving. You should have more cars than that!" We acquired three limousines and a Lincoln Town Car. Business was sweet for a couple of years—thanks in no small part to Michael Jackson himself, who had become a true fan of our service. He hired CLS to tour with and manage transportation for the Jackson 5 Victory Tour, which was launched to capitalize on the colossal success of *Thriller*. I sent my roommate, a UCLA grad named Derrick Vaughn, to manage that job.

We did very well for a couple of years. And then, almost as quickly as he had come in, my new partner disappeared. Or rather, "lost interest," as his business manager told me. In the entertainment business, there is no clearer way to say it. Irving was out, and I was told I needed to find somebody to take him out financially. I was 25. I didn't know anyone else, so just like that, Irving's people came and picked up the cars. I was left standing with $10,000 cash, half a million in canceled checks from various celebrities, and no cars.

But there was one thing I hadn't lost. I still had Michael Jackson as a client, and he was scheduled for a pickup that very night. You don't just tell the biggest star in the world that you don't have a car anymore. That would have been the end.

I remembered seeing one of our old limousines parked at a car lot down on Santa Monica Boulevard, around 12th Street. I went down there with my ten grand and that stack of canceled checks—proof that I could generate business. "Here's the situation," I told the owner. "I need the keys to that limo right now. We can work out the details when I get back." Maybe it was desperation in my voice, or maybe he just saw something in those checks, but he handed over the keys.

That single car became the foundation of everything that followed. I kept my rock stars, and I kept getting them whatever they needed. Every week, we were driving bands like Ratt, Warrant, The Police, XTC—whoever was coming through Southern California. We'd bring our bill to the closeout at night and get paid in cash, sometimes $3,500 to $5,000 per show.

The promoters began to trust me. The stars began to request me specifically. This time, I was building something real.

* * *

The collapse of my partnerships, first with Eli and then with Irving, taught me something crucial, though it would take years for the lesson to sink in.

In this business, being great at service isn't enough.

I was focused on making sure every client was happy and on solving every problem that came up. But I had no idea what was happening with the actual business. I didn't understand the paperwork I was signing. I didn't grasp the implications of various business structures. I didn't even know what questions I should be asking.

The truth was, I was still operating like a glorified chauffeur.

I knew how to make a rock star happy, handle a crisis, and turn a ride into an unforgettable experience. But I didn't know how to build a sustainable business, think beyond the next pickup, or protect myself.

Business relationships aren't just about making people feel special. They're about contracts, guarantees, and protecting yourself when things go wrong. But in those early years, I was still the kid trying to please his absent father. I became very good at delivering service.

I was also finding myself being pulled, ever more effortlessly, into a lifestyle that mirrored those of the people I was serving. At night, after the shows, my buddies and I would take that cash and hire a Learjet. We'd fly to Vegas, party all night, then come back just in time for the next round of pickups.

Beach Boys co-founder Carl Wilson (brother of fellow bandmates Brian and Dennis) told me that they used to call me in the middle of the night, and I would be half-cracked out of my mind. He said they were never sure if the car would show up the next morning. But no matter what condition I was in at night, I was always in the car the next morning, ready to drive.

It was a dangerous game, and I was playing it at full speed.

RISE
1987-1995

Seven years after starting with one car and a $20 investment, I had a real company.

And a real cocaine problem.

In 1987, after even Carl Wilson told me I was looking beyond rough, I called my grandmother and told her I needed money for rehab. Mercifully, she didn't hesitate.

The Betty Ford Center was different back then. It meant something. It also cost $5,000 for thirty days. I checked in, and I spent the first two weeks there with one of my clients: Eddie Van Halen.

The counselors didn't handle me with kid gloves. They told me I was just a glorified servant, a glorified chauffeur. I didn't like hearing that, but maybe I needed to be humbled a little.

I was scared shitless and desperate to get out of there. I even considered calling my airplane guy—the one who said he could get a helicopter, land it on the rehab's meadow, and fly me out. But he told me my mom had instructed him to leave me there.

I got out, made my amends, and went back to work. The industry welcomed me back. But I was about to enter a new phase, one that would test all I thought I knew about success and excess.

* * *

By 1988, I understood the limousine business. I was driving David Bowie, Bono, you name it. I was in good standing in the industry and doing very well. I was starting to realize that anyone could drive a car from point A to point B, but the magic happened when you could create something valuable out of thin air. What I didn't understand was that I was about to enter a world where money meant nothing and everything at the same time.

This crystallized for me one night with Bono. In 1987, U2 was already one of the biggest bands in the world, but Bono was still Bono—curious, engaged, almost boyish in his enthusiasm for music and musicians. I was tasked with taking him and his wife,

Ali, to dinner in Santa Monica. They had no idea where to go, so I suggested Guido's. During the ride, Bono and I fell into easy conversation—we were the same age, both twenty-seven, though living very different lives.

*My friend Phil and me with Bono and Larry from U2
(New Orleans, late '80s).*

He started telling me about all the famous people he'd met. He then mentioned, almost wistfully, that he'd never met Quincy Jones.

My ears perked up. In this business, you learn to listen for these moments—the casual mention of an unmet desire. While they were eating dinner, I slipped away and called Quincy.

"Q," I said, "I've got Bono from U2 in the car."

"Bring him by," Quincy said immediately. He was like that—always open to meeting other artists, ready to welcome someone new into his orbit.

After dinner, as I was driving them back toward the Sunset Marquis, I made my play. "Hey, let me show you some of these cool houses in Bel-Air," I said. They agreed, probably to be polite. We drove through the winding streets, past one mansion after another, until we reached Quincy's place at the top of Bel-Air Road.

"I need to use the restroom," I said casually. "This is actually a friend's house. Want to come see it? It's beautiful."

"No, that's okay. We'll wait here," Bono said, ever polite.

"No, really, you've got to see this house."

They got out of the car, still having no idea what was coming. When Quincy opened the door, Bono's face was priceless—sudden understanding, then pure amazement. Here was the man he'd just mentioned wanting to meet, standing in a doorway like a genie conjured from a lamp.

"Bono, this is Quincy Jones," I said, trying to keep my voice casual. "Quincy, this is my friend Bono and his wife, Ali."

They greeted each other like old friends, and we walked into Quincy's candlelit living room, which had a spectacular view of Los Angeles below.

"What are you working on, man?" Quincy asked, settling into his role as elder statesman of music.

Bono lit up. "I'm working on this record, *Rattle and Hum*," he said. "There's this track, 'When Love Comes to Town,' with B.B. King…"

"Let me hear it," Quincy said.

Without hesitation, Bono jumped up and began singing. Not a casual performance—he gave it everything, like he was on stage at Madison Square Garden instead of in a living room in Bel-Air. His voice filled the space, powerful and raw, while the candles flickered and the city lights danced below.

(**Note:** Quincy later put out an album called *Q's Juke Joint,* where he recounts the same story almost word for word on the back of the album cover.)

It was one of those moments you can't plan for. You can only create the conditions and hope something magical happens. They've been friends ever since.

That's what set me apart in this business. Anyone could drive a car or make dinner reservations. But understanding how to connect the dots between people—that was the real art of what we did.

It helped, of course, to be open to whatever it was that these megastars were going to throw at you. You seriously never knew what would happen—but when whatever was going to happen, did happen, *and* you took it in stride—that was a surefire way to endear yourself to clients.

One time, I picked up Elizabeth Taylor. She stepped out of her house, those famous violet eyes giving the car a once-over. Then, out of nowhere, she asked, "Are you hungry? We're making grilled shrimp."

When I went to peel the shrimp she'd offered, she stopped me. "No, no," she said. "That's the American way. You eat them whole."

There I was—being taught how to eat shrimp by one of the biggest stars in the world. But really, it wasn't so strange.

Everyone wants to connect—even people who seem to have everything.

Michael Jackson, Liz Taylor, and me at a Bruce Springsteen concert (Los Angeles, 1986).

* * *

While I was becoming the guy who could solve any problem for any rock star, I was also trying to build something that money couldn't buy: a real life.

That's when Lauren Bennett came back into my world. I'd known her sister in junior high and high school. Both were beautiful, and both were way out of my league back then. But now I had a little money, a position, and a growing company. I thought I knew what I was doing.

Getting Lauren to go out with me wasn't easy. She kept turning me down until I played my ace. "Hey, you want to go see Michael Jackson? He's playing the Sports Arena tonight." Her friends told me later they'd said, "It's Michael Jackson—fuck yeah, go with him!"

But I didn't just take her to see the concert. When we got to the Sports Arena, I drove down the back ramp where my guys were waiting. They opened the gates, and I drove right underneath the building. Lauren had no idea what was happening until we were being shown into Michael's dressing room.

"Oh, Charlie, is this the one you've been talking about?" Michael asked kindly. The look on Lauren's face was priceless. When I took her home that night, I asked if she wanted to go again the next night. He was playing another show, and I still had to work. She didn't hesitate.

We started dating seriously. Eventually, we started talking about moving in together. Her father, though, wasn't having it. "I'm not letting my daughter live with you," he said. "Why buy the cow when you're getting the milk for free?"

Point taken. We got engaged. And in 1990, we got married at the Beverly Hills Hotel. Three hundred and fifty guests, mostly her family's Vegas and L.A. connections—her father was in the casino interior design business. Joe Walsh, John Entwistle, and Victoria Principal came from my side. Instead of going to Africa for our honeymoon, we bought our first house in Westchester.

Lauren was working for the Ritz Carlton as a salesperson. They were opening a new hotel in Marina del Rey, and she was handling pre-sales. I'd never had a hotel contract; at that point, we were strictly a rock-and-roll outfit. But I wanted this one. Not just because it was Lauren's hotel, but because I could see how it could change our whole operation.

The general manager seemed like a cool guy. He liked to ride motorcycles. So I did what the rock-and-roll world had taught me: I bought him a Harley Davidson. Just showed up one day and said, "This is yours. We want to be your limousine company. Let's be pals."

Looking back, it was excessive, gratuitous. But getting that hotel account changed everything. They made us go through their orientation program, the same one all their employees took. That's where we learned their philosophy: "We are ladies and gentlemen serving ladies and gentlemen."

We took everything we learned from the Ritz and applied it to CLS. Their standards became our standards. We weren't just driving rock stars anymore: we were building something professional, something that could last. Something I could be proud to show Lauren's father.

I was trying to become the kind of man who deserved the stability Lauren represented. But I was still the guy who'd learned everything I knew from rock stars and late nights. Sometimes, those two worlds didn't mix as well as I hoped. But at that point, there was still room to learn and grow—and plenty of money to be made.

* * *

By 1993, I thought I had gotten a good handle on luxury service. I had driven everyone in the entertainment business, handled million-dollar deals, and fulfilled impossible demands. But I was about to learn that everything I knew about high-end service was just the beginning.

One of my drivers had befriended Victor Lin, who was head of security at the Beverly Hills Hotel. Victor was the liaison for the Royal Family of Brunei, who owned the hotel.

"Would you like to be the transportation for the Royal Family?" he asked during our first meeting. The way he said it made it sound simple, like he was offering me a regular corporate account. I said I'd give him 20% of whatever he gave me. He agreed, and I thought I'd just landed another good client.

I had no idea I was stepping into a different world entirely.

My first job was in Florida, handling transportation for the two sons of Prince Jeffrey, brother to the Sultan of Brunei. His sons were Prince Hakeem, who was 21, and Prince Bahar, who was 12. They each had their own G4s—one canary yellow, the other royal purple—and they'd flown into West Palm Beach because young Prince Hakeem was buying a couple of Sikorsky S-76 helicopters to take back to Brunei.

The young prince, it turned out, was already a 2,000-hour Cobra gunship pilot. His father had agreed to let him buy these two helicopters for $6 million, but only if he could pass his pilot's exam in the United States. While he was busy with that, we were handling transportation for his entourage.

That's when I got my first real lesson in royal service. When the Royals moved into the Four Seasons, they took over the entire top floor. The elevator doors opened to a hallway lined with hotel rooms, each occupied by a member of the entourage. I had seen plenty of stars' riders and requirements by that point, but this was different. It was simply how this family lived.

Everything I thought I knew about service had to be recalibrated. With rock stars, you could sometimes say no if something was impossible. With the Royal Family, that word didn't exist in the vocabulary. You never said no. You said, "I'll see what I can do." Then you made it happen, no matter what it took.

Here's a good example. What do you think happens when a young prince decides, well after closing time, that he needs a Quarter Pounder with Cheese?

It was two in the morning in West Palm Beach when I got that call. I stared at the darkened McDonald's across the street from the Four Seasons. The security man who'd delivered this request stood waiting, as if I could materialize fast food from thin air.

So what did I do? I called the hotel general manager.

"Do you have any idea what time it is?" he cried, furious.

"Do you have any idea what losing the Royal Family would cost you?" I countered. "Fifty thousand dollars a night. I need you to get that McDonald's open."

The dominoes fell. The hotel manager called the police chief, who called the McDonald's owner. By the time I delivered that Quarter Pounder—which, by now, had cost $250,000 to procure—the prince had fallen asleep.

His security guard unwrapped it and took a big bite. I asked if I needed to go back and get another. I did not.

To quiet the local outrage over opening a McDonald's at 2 a.m. for a burger, we donated another quarter-million dollars to local charities. Half a million dollars for a Quarter Pounder. And nobody in the royal entourage batted an eye.

Money meant nothing and everything in their world. Princess Jafri would spend days shopping at Cartier, Tiffany, David Yurman—but you'd never see a shopping bag. The next day, fifteen car service vehicles would appear with red Cartier bags, another fifteen with blue Tiffany boxes. When it was time to leave, they'd call me: "We need a cargo plane. And 150 Samsonite suitcases."

The money for these sprees came directly from the Federal Reserve, but even that was a production. They wouldn't touch used bills. Everything had to be new, sequential numbers, like peeling bills off a notepad. Mr. Robert would arrive with his signature accessory, a satchel containing Johnny Walker Blue Label and a crystal glass, to oversee the transaction.

Literally nothing was off limits to them. When the Sultan of Brunei met with the King of Jordan in Orlando, Florida, I was told that they needed their three bulletproof Mercedes-Benz sedans, which were parked in Los Angeles, brought to Florida. I had three days to get them there. Impossible by road.

And yet, there was a way—of course there was a way. Down I went to Federal Express with the Gold Coast company name and, well, they loaded the cars directly onto a DC-10. Nobody blinked. And off the cars flew to Florida.

When they asked me to pick up $20 million in cash arriving from London, I learned the choreography of power. First, find the civilian customs agent and provide a generous envelope. When the military customs agent appears, play it cool. The duffel bags come out. Three million dollars weighs about ninety pounds. Load them like they're gym clothes.

Their security detail, the Gurkhas, were warriors who stood guard 24/7. To them, dying to protect the Royal Family would be an honor. You didn't mess with the Gurkhas. You didn't mess with anything in this world.

Even their rules about personal property were absolute. If you left a pair of gloves in a car that transported a princess, those gloves were now property of the Royal Family. You couldn't ask for them back. They had crossed an invisible line into their realm.

I had gone from driving rock stars to serving actual royalty. The transition taught me something I couldn't have learned any other way: excess has no ceiling. There's always another level of wealth, of privilege—of absurdity.

* * *

The money to be made from all these theatrics, of course, was extraordinary. But unfortunately, it didn't last.

When Mr. Mustafa, my connection to the family, died, it was over, just like that. Doesn't matter how good you are. When your connection dies, someone else gets to do what you were doing. Someone else gets to learn about quarter-million-dollar hamburgers and sequential bills.

But by the time the Royals and I parted ways in 1995, my business had gone from $1 million to $10 million a year.

Naturally, my ambitions grew alongside my revenue. And I saw the obvious next step: I needed to expand.

PEAK
1995-2000

By 1995, I had L.A. figured out.

But I noticed something about my L.A. clients. When they weren't in the cars, at point A, or at point B, they all seemed to live on airplanes. Especially planes headed to New York.

The transcontinental boogie, we called it: leave L.A. on Sunday, head back from New York on Friday. I was watching this pattern, watching all this business going to other companies, and thinking: *Why not me?*

I started in New York with one car. Just one, like I had in L.A. fifteen years earlier. Within twelve months, we had fifteen cars on the road. The rock bands that trusted us in L.A. started using us in New York. Having my brother run the operation meant I didn't even have to be there. I could focus on building relationships while he handled the day-to-day.

But the real game-changer came through an unexpected breakfast at the Four Seasons in New York. I was there with Lauren during another Royal Family visit, and Richard Von Adler, the general manager, was having coffee nearby. Lauren, with her Ritz-Carlton background, pushed me to say hello. I didn't want to; he'd turned us down before, choosing Manhattan Limousine instead.

But I went over, and that conversation changed everything. "How badly do you want my hotel?" he asked me. He'd just been to Hong Kong, where the Chinese owners of the Four Seasons had their fleet of Mercedes-Benz sedans. It looked so elegant, professional, worlds apart from the standard Lincoln Town Cars every other service used.

"I'll give you this hotel," he said, "if you'll operate with a dedicated fleet of Mercedes-Benz sedans."

The math was daunting. Each Mercedes cost $25,000 more than a Lincoln. But as I'd learned from all these power players over the years, sometimes, you have to make the big play. When an opportunity to throw your weight lands in front of you, sometimes, you've got to show you're willing and able to step up and take it.

"I'll buy you twenty," I said. Obviously, I had no idea how I'd pay for them.

Von Adler had to give his existing service company the chance to match the offer. But when he called me in Palm Beach the following Monday, the deal was mine. I had ninety days to make it happen.

A young banker named Ryan Easton at Comerica Bank saw the potential. With the Four Seasons contract in hand, they gave me a $2 million credit line. And just like that, we changed the face of luxury transportation in Manhattan. Nobody had ever put an all-Mercedes fleet on the streets of New York.

Then Canali got involved. The Italian suit company wanted our drivers in their black suits so badly that they made it worth our while. Suddenly, we had chauffeurs in custom suits driving Mercedes-Benz sedans. The whole image of car service in New York shifted overnight.

The effect was instant. The Chinese owners also had the Four Seasons in Beverly Hills, and Beverly Hills wanted what New York had. Then came the Beverly Wilshire. The Beverly Hills Hotel, still owned by the Brunei people, dropped the company that had replaced me and came back. The St. Regis in New York followed. Within six weeks, we had added about $10 million in new business.

That's when I understood that we were no longer just a car service. We were a brand.

In New York, L.A., anywhere: if you were somebody, if you had real money and wanted the best, you had a CLS account. We weren't cheap, but that was the point. Having our card in your wallet meant something.

Looking back, New York taught me that success comes down to understanding what luxury really means to people.

Those Mercedes weren't just cars. They were statements.

Those Canali suits weren't just clothes. They were promises.

We were selling an experience, a feeling, a membership in something exclusive. That lesson would serve me well as we expanded into other markets.

* * *

Then came NetJets.

The NetJets deal came through a chance meeting with Richard Santulli and Casey Wasserman, grandson of Hollywood legend Lew Wasserman. Over breakfast at the Beverly Hills Hotel, it became clear that NetJets and CLS shared the same understanding of high-end service. They wanted our celebrity connections; we wanted their elite client base. A perfect match.

I was already doing about a million dollars a year with them when Santulli called personally. By then, Warren Buffett had bought NetJets for $700 million, and Santulli had built what looked like NASA's mission control in Columbus, Ohio: a $40 million facility dedicated to private aviation.

"I've got a problem," Santulli said. "I want to throw Carey Limousine out of here. I didn't realize you weren't doing all my business."

I was in my Gulfstream within hours, heading to Columbus. The irony wasn't lost on me, flying my own private jet to bid on handling all of NetJets' ground transportation. But by then, that was my world. Eight million dollars of new business? Sure, I could handle that. I always said yes first and figured out the details later.

The meeting room looked exactly like what you'd expect when you're dealing with Berkshire Hathaway money—leather chairs, glass walls, people in suits who looked like they calculated risk in their sleep. Richard Smith, the president under Santulli, had assembled his entire team to vet me.

I could feel it immediately. They thought I was too small. They wanted to "stair-step" me into the business, test the waters, move slowly. All the things that careful, sensible businesspeople do.

But I knew something they didn't. Carey had transgressed—unforgivably. They had hired away one of NetJets' employees, trying to get into the private jet business themselves. They'd violated an unwritten rule: you don't compete with your clients.

After my meeting with Richard Smith and the NetJets, I called Mr. Santulli and told him what Carey had done. I was told to go back into the office and wait for Mr. Smith.

Soon Santulli's message came down through Richard Smith—"If any of you dumb motherfuckers can't figure out that we're using CLS, you're fired"—it felt like validation of everything I'd built. In seconds, I went from being too small to handle their business to being the only one who could handle it. Getting things done with the boss "top down" is a much better business model than trying to win over the middle managers.

That contract pushed us past $10 million a year with them alone. By 2000, I had operations in Los Angeles, New York, Las Vegas, San Francisco, and Aspen. Seven hundred cars, $70 million dollars a year in revenue.

I had the entirety of the rock and roll industry locked up. I was getting huge chunks of the film industry, just by association. I had multiple hotel properties and alliances. Major inroads into corporate industry. Across entertainment, business, hotels, even royalty—these people knew my name, and they respected me.

I had the world by the balls.

* * *

And how was my lifestyle looking?

Well. Listen.

I owned a family home in Brentwood Park. Two houses in Malibu Colony. Two in Las Vegas and two ranches in Texas.

I owned too many Ferraris to count.

I owned three private jets: a Gulfstream II SP, a Lear 31, and a fractional share in a Citation X.

I had chauffeured cars. Staff. My son Hunter and daughter Quinn each had a nanny.

I also had connections in all kinds of worlds by then. Here's just one example. Through a charity event, I'd gotten involved with the Naval Special Warfare Center in Coronado, across the bay from downtown San Diego. When one of their guys died in a training accident, John Paul Mitchell and I helped fund the memorial. They wanted to spread his ashes on Mount McKinley.

After that, I got to know some of the guys from SEAL Team 3. They invited me to their training sessions when I'd come out on my 42-foot Fountain boat to San Diego. The second time I went to Coronado, they asked if I wanted to join their qualification swim, a mile in the open ocean. "Don't worry," they told me, "you don't even need to know how to swim. We'll be right there."

I watched them dive in two by two, like dolphins. I was more afraid of letting someone else drive my boat than I was about swimming with them, so I stayed behind and drove my boat. By the time I got my boat back to the dock, they were already showered and ready to go. A young SEAL named Chris Kyle—years before he became the famous "American Sniper"—was part of that team. He even came to my fortieth birthday party at the house in Brentwood.

This was pre-9/11, before everything changed for those guys. Looking back, it feels like a different world.

Here's the point: by 2000, I was forty years old, and I felt invincible.

* * *

After twenty years of building my limousine empire, I finally had enough money to indulge my deepest passion.

Growing up, I'd devoured every issue of *Western Horseman* magazine, memorizing the names of world champions and dreaming about the rodeo life. Now, I could do more than just dream.

I'd been going to the National Finals Rodeo in Las Vegas since 1986. Now, I had the clout and the cash to embed myself in that world. Through a charity event—the Ben Johnson rodeo they used to have in Burbank—I met Tuff Hedeman, a world champion bull rider and a legend in the sport. Tuff introduced me to his friend Jim Sharp, another world champion, and they brought me into their circle. He even introduced me to Lane

Frost, the legendary bull rider who was killed at Cheyenne later that summer. These types of guys were my heroes, and I got to meet them all.

I started sponsoring cowboys at the National Finals, putting their names and likenesses on my limousines. Just picture that: ten stretch limos cruising the Strip, world champions' faces emblazoned on the sides.

But that was just the beginning. Pretty soon, I was flying Ty Murray—basically the Michael Jordan of rodeo—and other champions around in my Gulfstream during Cowboy Christmas. Cowboy Christmas refers to two weeks around the Fourth of July, when there are something like 700 rodeos across the country. These guys would try to hit as many as they could, racing from one to the next to rack up prize money.

Before I came along, they were doing it the hard way: driving themselves, exhausted, trying to make it to the next show. But with my plane, we could do two, sometimes three rodeos in a day. Reno to Greeley, Colorado; down to El Paso; then up to Cody, Wyoming—the Gulfstream made it possible.

I went all in, as I always did. Three rigs with drivers and four horse trailers strategically placed around the country. Two planes at our disposal. I spent probably half a million that first year just on horses, trailers, and equipment.

The funny thing was, through all this, I had an agenda.

In my mind, I wasn't just supporting this sport. I was going to be part of it.

I actually thought I could compete, you know? These world champions were teaching me to team rope, and I figured that was enough. I remember being at Tuff's place in Texas, looking at his arena, and thinking, *how hard could it be?* There's a header on the left, a heeler on the right, and a steer in the middle. The header ropes the horns, turns left, and the heeler catches the back feet. Simple!

I'd done some trick riding as a kid, and I knew how to handle a rope. First time out, I actually caught one leg, and man, I was hooked.

But catching one leg in practice, as I learned, was about as far from being a real competitor as driving a car is from running a transportation empire. But that was me: always thinking I could jump right to the top of anything I tried.

Looking back, I can see that the rodeo world gave me something the limo business couldn't. In the transportation world, I was the guy who could make anything happen, who could solve any problem with enough money and connections. But in rodeo, you couldn't buy your way to being good. These guys had been doing it their whole lives, and they had a kind of authenticity that all my success couldn't touch.

Maybe that's what I was really chasing.

Here I am at the rodeo (Salinas, Calif. 2003).

I made the cover of *Professional Pilot* (above) at the height of CLS's success. Behind me are my private jet, my pilot, my sales manager, my CFO, and chief mechanic (2001). *Los Angeles Times* article (image that follows, July 1996).

I ended up buying a 500-acre ranch in Texas, right next to Tuff's spread. Then, I bought another 90-acre place that I gave to my daughter. Remember, this was on top of the houses in Malibu Colony, Brentwood Park, and Vegas. But the ranch was something different. It was my attempt to be part of this world I'd admired since I was a kid.

I started hosting something called the Hork Dog Roping at my place in Vegas. Picture this: a real team roping arena in my backyard, world champions dropping by like it was the neighborhood barbecue. During National Finals week, I'd have fifty cowboys staying at my place, their horse trailers parked all around the property.

Ty Murray tried to help me understand what I was getting into. One day at a rodeo, after he'd won all three of his events—because that's what Ty did—he told me to get on his horse and take the victory lap. The rodeo producers were furious. Here's the greatest all-around champion in the sport, and some wannabe is running his victory lap. Ty just looked at me and said, "Whatever you do, don't fall off." That was Ty: he could make you feel included while reminding you exactly where you stood.

The crazy thing was, I was spending as much time chasing rodeo as I was running my company. More, probably. My business was doing $70 million a year, but in my head, I was a cowboy. I'd be on the phone doing million-dollar deals between rounds at some local roping competition. Looking back, I can see how that split focus was part of what led to my problems later.

But the rodeo world gave me something real, even if I never became the competitor I dreamed of being. These guys—Tuff,

Ty, Lane Frost before he was killed—they became my true friends. When I went to prison years later, Tuff was one of the only people outside my family who came to visit. That tells you something about the kind of people they are.

I ended up introducing Ty to his future wife, Jewel. Atlantic Records called asking if I could host her at one of the rodeos. I couldn't use Tuff because he was married, but Ty was single. Six months later, Ty called to tell me they were dating. They ended up together for 16 years.

* * *

But no amount of connections could make me into a real rodeo cowboy. Nor could all my savvy, drive, and cash flow steer me smoothly through the realities of business.

Success at the level I had reached required a different kind of infrastructure. NetJets flew into every major city in America. We needed affiliates everywhere, and those affiliates needed to be paid.

My company, which had started with one car, was now orchestrating a nationwide network of vendors, all of whom needed to deliver at the highest level.

At first, we managed it beautifully. But as we grew, the cracks started to show. NetJets clients would call us for service, but increasingly, we couldn't pay our vendors fast enough. A company called Savoya saw the opportunity. They'd pay vendors immediately, taking our business piece by piece. They'd go to the same vendors we used in Texas or Chicago, and while we were asking for 30-day terms, they were paying on the spot.

It was a lesson I should have learned from my early days with Irving Azoff. In this business, relationships aren't enough. You need systems, infrastructure, and financial stability.

But I was still operating on instinct and a relentless desire to please. I would still say yes to everything and figure out the details later.

It worked—until it didn't.

FALL
2000-2012

In 2000, it still seemed that everything I touched turned to gold. I was in L.A., New York, Las Vegas, San Francisco, and Aspen. Seven hundred cars across the country pulling in $70 million a year.

My marriage to Lauren was still solid on paper. We had the kids, the homes, the cars, the boats. A life most people would envy. All the trappings of success.

But something was missing. And I have to admit that I wasn't smart enough to figure out what it was or leave well enough alone.

That's when Elena walked into my life. It happened at dinner with Casey Wasserman and his wife, Laura. Elena was with them, recently divorced from a studio head, Michael Carrington. She had three kids of her own, around the same age as my own.

Something about her just lit up the room. Looking back, I can see all the warning signs. But at the time, all I could see was her.

That Christmas, we were headed to Hawaii, staying at the Four Seasons Hualalai on the Big Island. Elena just happened to show up there with a friend. I can still remember the moment everything changed. I was sitting with Elena in that infinity pool that looks out over the ocean, and it struck me like a lightning bolt—I was in love with her. Or I thought I was. My wife had warned me not to spend time with Elena at the resort, but by then, I wasn't listening to anyone's warnings. Frankly, when you're successful enough, you start thinking the normal rules don't apply to you.

Things moved fast after that. By Valentine's Day, Elena and I were meeting in Las Vegas. When spring break came around, I told Lauren I had some business bullshit in New York. Instead, I took Elena on the Citation X. She had this beautiful Prada bag that was really a portable martini set. We got smashed and flew across the country together. We spent four days in New York, where I bought her an 11-carat sapphire emerald cut stone from GRAFF set in Platinum.

When I got back from that spring break trip, Lauren and I went to dinner. She looked at me and said, "It seems like you don't want to be married anymore." She didn't know about Elena—at least, I didn't think she did—but she knew something was wrong.

I just looked back at her and said, "Yeah, you're right. I just don't feel it anymore."

We went through the motions of therapy, but how can therapy work when one person is straight-up lying? I was keeping a trunk full of secrets from her, and I was too arrogant and scared to even do *that* well.

Looking back, I should have been honest with her. She deserved that much. But I was still playing everything like it was a business deal: figure out the angles, minimize the losses.

Nevada's divorce laws worked in my favor. You can be divorced there in six weeks, compared to California, where it can drag on forever. I knew if I got divorced in California, I'd get destroyed on child support alone. It would have been as much as the property settlement. So I made sure it happened in Nevada. Lauren went along with it, probably just wanting it all over and done.

The settlement was millions. Plus, she got to live in the Malibu house for a year before finding her own place. But here's where it got complicated. When the year was up, I owed her a significant amount of money, and a lot of my liquidity was tied up in the equity of that Malibu house. I'd bought it for $3.7 million, and by then it was worth $5.8 million. So I offered her a deal: she could keep the house if it counted for $2 million of what I owed her.

Looking back, I probably should have just sold the house then. But that was me, always thinking I knew better, always looking for the clever solution. Lauren, of course, was smarter about money than I ever was. She held onto that house until 2015, then sold it (I was told) for around $12 million.

She was always more practical, more grounded. After the sale, she bought a double-wide in Paradise Cove and got into triathlons. She knew who she was. I was still trying to be somebody I wasn't.

The divorce agreement had me paying her $60,000 to $70,000 a month. And at the time, even that didn't seem like a big deal. The money was flowing, and I thought it always would.

* * *

9/11 hit. And the business completely fell off the map.

No one could fly. The rich and famous in L.A. and New York continued using the car services. But Vegas was a tourist town, and when the tourists disappeared, it was like someone had cut the lights.

And I was still on the hook for countless payments. From a new million-dollar engine for my Gulf Stream to my bills from the NetJets affiliates to Lauren's monthly payments to my weekends playing cowboy. Everything just kept churning along, even though the bottom was very clearly starting to fall out.

I couldn't ignore it: I needed serious investment to keep CLS running.

The investment bankers arrived like sharks, smelling blood. Daggerhorn Capital saw something in the business that they liked. Maybe the celebrity clients, maybe the contracts.

They gave me $20 million. Three million bought them eight percent of the company. The rest was a loan.

Did I manage that loan responsibly? Of course not.

Instead of paying off the banks that were about to foreclose, I paid the vendors I owed in the limousine industry. I took care of my friends.

The banks, of course, didn't care about my friends. They foreclosed. And Daggerhorn Capital? They didn't save me. Instead, they took over. They cut my salary from three million to six hundred thousand a year. That might sound like a lot to you, but it was barely enough to cover the jet payments and nowhere near enough for my lifestyle.

In hindsight, I could have hired a CEO who had a handle on managing investment banker partners, and had run a company of similar size and with similar problems. But that solution went against every instinct I'd ever had. I was used to running my company as my own piggy bank, and I wasn't going to stop now.

In 2004, just to showcase my spite at their attempts to curtail my spending, I rented Mel Brooks' house in Malibu for the summer for $70,000 a month and bought a new black convertible 360 Ferrari.

"You don't roast marshmallows while Rome is burning," they told me.

"Fuck you guys," I told them.

They knew I was a drug addict. They took me to lunch and told me that I needed to go to rehab. Even then, I didn't take the deal. I couldn't bear admitting I was so out of control.

So what did they do? They took me out to dinner, and they told me I was "out."

The sad part is that all I had to do was admit my shortcomings. They could have worked out some kind of exit deal after I went to rehab. But since I was lying about my addiction, it was easier for them to just get rid of me.

And remember my one-time partner, Irving, who was in until he was out? Same deal. Out meant done. Finished.

And it was fair enough. Their cash infusions had now driven their ownership stake from 8% to 50%. Now they could fire me, and they sure as hell did. I spent a whole afternoon in a boardroom, going from desk to desk, signing my name what seemed like hundreds of times.

They offered to let me keep the Las Vegas operation if I'd go to rehab and leave quietly. What choice did I have? It was better than the alternative: getting thrown out on my ass with nothing to show for it.

When I got out of rehab in November 2004, I no longer owned CLS New York or CLS L.A. My life was now all about Las Vegas.

* * *

Las Vegas was a different animal from my California or New York businesses. Instead of celebrity clients and corporate accounts, we were dealing with tourists trying to get back to their hotels after a show.

Still, I knew how to make money there. CLS handled seventeen casino properties, which were our lifeline. Rather than handle their high-roller business, we basically became the alternative to taxis. You'd walk out of any casino, see the long cab line, slip the doorman twenty bucks, and he'd walk you over to one of our cars. Sixty dollars, and you could skip the wait. We might have twenty cars sitting at each hotel property.

But the strip clubs were where the real money moved. Here's how it worked: A group of five guys would want to hit a club. As mentioned, instead of waiting in the taxi line, they would slip the doorman a twenty and get into one of our waiting cars. The driver would bring them to a club, no charge—or so it seemed to the passenger. The club then paid us $80 per head for the patronage, so that was $400 for one car. The driver and doorman would split that, minus our $60 fee. Everybody won.

Then Niko Stavros, who owned a club called Olympic Gardens, came to me with a proposition. He wanted an exclusive deal, meaning that all our "neutral" customers would get dropped off at his club. By law, if someone got in the car asking for Sapphire's or another club, we had to take them there. But half the customers didn't have a preference. Those were the ones Niko wanted.

For directing that traffic his way, Niko paid me a personal check for a million dollars every year. On top of that, he still paid the per-head fee and took care of my drivers, the doormen, and everyone in the chain. By the time a customer walked through his door, Niko was in for about $175 before they'd spent a dime. But he was clearing $5 million a year after all the payouts, so it worked for everyone.

I ran this operation at night, making my rounds with my security guy—whose name, no joke, was "T-Money." We'd hit every hotel on the Strip, check in with the doormen, and make sure everything was running smoothly. We were moving 450–500 cars a week through Olympic Gardens alone.

The girls there treated me like a king: I was the guy who kept their money flowing. After Olympic Gardens, we'd hit Hayes Nightclub until four, then Crazy Horse until six in the morning. Then, home with whichever girls wanted to party, sleep it off, and do it all again the next night.

The million from Niko helped, but it wasn't enough to keep up with my lifestyle or cover the holes in the business.

The Vegas operation had been taking $12 million a year. From 2004, when it became my sole business, through 2007, it grew to $32 million a year.

I was turning into a true Vegas degenerate, but I was still running a transportation company.

* * *

Meanwhile, things had started to get really complicated with Elena. We had five kids between us, and in my head, I had seen this perfect *Brady Bunch* scenario. But reality had other plans.

From 2000 to 2006, we were on-again, off-again. Every round of on-again was more intense than the last. She could be brutal, but I was addicted to that intensity.

When we were off, I'd see Anya, a gorgeous masseuse from New Zealand. Anya was something else entirely. I'd walk into Mr. Chow's in Beverly Hills with her, and the paparazzi would start shooting, thinking she must be somebody famous. She wasn't. She was just that radiant.

But more than that, she was decent, genuine. Like my wife Megan today, Anya just loved me for who I was, not what I could provide.

But I couldn't see that then. I was too caught up in the drama with Elena.

Whenever things blew cold with Elena, I would see Anya. She was my constant, my escape. But that wasn't fair to her either. Elena would find out, and the cycle would start again. Meanwhile, I'm trying to keep my business from falling apart, dealing with the aftermath of 9/11, watching my Vegas operation hemorrhage money. But I couldn't stop the pattern.

Then Anya's visa situation complicated everything. She'd been out of status for ten years: an illegal alien, basically. But she had a life here, a house in West L.A., a little dog. I thought I could fix it the way I fixed everything else: by throwing money at it. I gave some guy $35,000 for what he promised would be a foolproof passport with an encrypted visa. Anya could have just gone to the Australian consulate, paid $3.75 for a new passport, gone home, and dealt with coming back legally. But that wasn't dramatic enough for us.

We took my Learjet to Cabo and had a great time. But when we tried to come back through Brownfield, Immigrations and

Customs Enforcement (ICE) was waiting. And ICE didn't play around. They just snatched her and started deportation proceedings.

Deportation doesn't happen in a day. It's a drawn-out, humiliating process. She went from being this beautiful, free spirit to being locked up in detention centers along the southern border. I spent weeks chasing her through the system and finally got them to deport her to Tijuana instead of New Zealand. I met her there, took her back to Cabo, rented a villa from a guy named Jimmy Page (not the rock star), and that's where we lived, on and off, from 2007 to 2012.

Anya was bipolar, though we didn't really understand that then. In the early 2000s, they were still figuring out how to treat it. Nothing seemed to work—except running and maybe cocaine.

Then, in the spring of 2012, I got married to a woman named Amber. We divorced six weeks later. For Anya, watching me marry Amber was the last straw. One day, she got a propane tank, put a bag over her head, ran a hose from the tank to the bag, duct-taped it around her neck, and ended it all. She was 42.

To this day, I feel responsible for that. I was living so recklessly, so selfishly. Anya was mentally ill, yes, but I made everything worse. My kids loved her. She was decent, and I treated her like a fallback option. That's something I have to live with.

*　*　*

While I was juggling women—and, by the way, still chasing my rodeo dreams—the foundation of everything I'd built was starting to crack. That's the thing about success. It can mask a lot of problems until suddenly it can't anymore.

By 2007, my Vegas operation was doing $32 million a year, and in my typical style, I was already spending the $50 million I thought was coming. The numbers looked good on paper, but I wasn't watching them closely enough. I was too busy flying world champion cowboys around in my Gulf Stream, hosting parties at my ranches, and trying to keep up with multiple households and multiple women.

Looking back, I can see how scattered my attention was. You can't run a multi-million-dollar operation like it's a side hustle. But that's exactly what I was doing. In one day, I might be making huge deals in the morning, flying to a rodeo competition in the afternoon, and ending up in Cabo with Anya by evening. When you're living that way, burning through money at that pace, you start to think the pipeline will never run dry.

But the business world doesn't care about your lifestyle or your distractions. It doesn't care that you've got world champions staying at your ranch or that you're trying to juggle relationships in three different countries. It just keeps moving, with or without your full attention. And in 2007, it was just on the precipice of moving in ways none of us saw coming.

* * *

In early 2008, when the Great Recession hit, President Obama went on TV and told people to watch their spending. Specifically, he warned viewers to think twice before spending all their cash in Las Vegas.

It was as if a faucet was turned off. Every convention scheduled for Vegas from spring 2008 on was canceled. Just like that, our revenue dropped by more than half.

But of course, our expenses didn't.

We needed at least $21 million a year just to cover overhead. By then, we had 230 cars, each one with payments, insurance, and maintenance. At the Mirage hotels, those twenty cars sitting at the ready all needed backing cash flow for payroll, fuel, and repairs. You can't just park half the fleet and wait for better times down the road. You have to keep feeding the operation, or everything collapses in on itself.

So that's where the business was. And frankly, that was just one part of an enormous complex of obligations. I still had all those planes, all those boats and cars, and divorce payments. And all those habits—the appetites, the drugs, the complex of friends and hangers-on who looked to me as someone who was always good for a wild time. I was completely enmeshed.

And now the collapse of the Vegas economy was starting to pull the thread that could unravel everything.

When the money slowed down, I had to get creative.

Looking back, I can see how each step led to the next one, how desperation turned into something totally indefensible. But at the time, I was just trying to keep it afloat.

The solution I came up with seemed brilliant at first—the kind of thinking that had always worked for me. We had 35,000 American Express cards in our database. This was before instant text notifications and real-time tracking. Back then, you'd use your card and wait for the bill to show up in the mail. That lag time—that float—became my obsession.

It started when Pam, my bookkeeper, came to me one Monday morning. We needed $350,000 to clear the checks she'd written, but we'd only brought in maybe $50,000. In the old days, I would have just moved money around and called in some favors. But given the slowdown in the whole environment, those options were gone.

Looking at that database of credit cards, I had what I thought was an inspired idea.

"Let's pick some cards at random," I told her. "Charge each one between $2,500 and $3,000." We'd get the money from American Express right away, clear the bank, and keep the operation running. The way I saw it, we had three weeks before the cardholders would even see the charges. By then, we'd have enough legitimate revenue to pay them back.

But of course, that's not how it worked out.

The phone calls started coming in: "We didn't spend $3,500 with you. We spent $350!" No problem, I thought. We'd just charge another set of cards to cover the refunds.

It became a Ponzi scheme, pure and simple. New charges were used to cover the refunds from the old ones. Every day, we were juggling more balls, going deeper into the hole.

American Express finally caught on. They shut down our merchant number: a disaster in Vegas, where almost everyone carries an AmEx. The funny thing was, out of the $5.2 million we'd run through this scheme, $1.8 million in charges were never disputed. People just paid them. Maybe they couldn't remember what they'd spent in Vegas, or maybe the amounts were small enough that they didn't consider them worth fighting. In any event, we somehow managed—like magic—to take nearly $2 million in what were essentially unauthorized loans. In other words, stealing.

But it wasn't enough, so I kept on going. If anything, losing the American Express operation just made me more desperate, more creative. That's when I discovered you could cash payroll checks at any casino in Vegas. As in, they acted like a bank: you hand over the check, they hand you back the cash.

Of course the casinos cashed payroll checks. They're hoping you'll gamble the money before you leave!

So, just like that, I started printing checks for my drivers and then sending them to different casinos to cash them. I'd send them out with five different checks each, amounts varying from $2,500 to $3,500. They'd cash them, bring back the money, and we'd use it to cover the bank. The next day, we'd do it all again.

The banks were okay with me over-drafting in the morning so long as we covered it by two in the afternoon. Every day became a shell game: figuring out how much we needed by one in the morning and calculating how many drivers we'd have to send out. Some days, it was $50,000, others as much as $280,000.

I told myself I just had to hold on until the economy got better. But I didn't know anything about economics, or cycles, or how long a downturn could last. I was just a guy who had always been able to fix problems by being clever, finding the angle.

My relationship with the Vegas casinos had always been complicated. They loved me when I was bringing in high rollers and looked the other way when I was floating checks. I had credit lines everywhere. Michael Gaughan, owner of the South Point Casino, was practically family. I'd known him since my days with Lauren. But even friendship has limits when you're passing bad checks.

By the time the FBI finally came for me, I had about $175,000 in checks floating at South Point and another $80,000 with Boyd Gaming.

The bank president had tried to warn me. He called me in one day and asked why I was paying my personal assistant

$350,000 a year, why mechanics were making $120,000, why my drivers were far and away the best-paid drivers in the entire city. Of course, these were from all the payroll checks we were floating through the casinos.

I looked at him with all the entitlement and arrogance I had left. "I don't see how it's any of your fucking business what I do with my money."

Well, it *was* their business. The bank was on the FDIC watch list. If I went down, I might take them with me.

They could see it. And so could everyone else; it's Vegas, and word travels fast.

But me? I didn't—couldn't—stop.

I was still gambling, still flying to my ranch, still trying to live like nothing had changed. I'd built this image of myself: part transportation mogul, part rodeo cowboy. And I couldn't let go of either one. When you're used to solving every problem by throwing money at it, it's hard to admit when the money's running out.

* * *

But on December 13, 2012, everything changed.

I know the exact time because the digital clock by my bed flashed in the darkness as I jolted awake. For a moment, I thought it was an earthquake. Then I heard Terrell, aka T-Money, shouting from the other side of the house.

The second explosion took out my front door. Blew it right off its hinges.

If you've never seen a tactical team breach a house, it's just like in the movies—only faster, louder, and more violent. And suddenly, your bedroom is full of men in black body armor, rifles raised.

"FBI! On the ground! Now!"

I was in my underwear. The floor was cold. Someone was shouting about a warrant. Beyond my bedroom window, I could see more agents swarming across my property, tactical vehicles on my lawn, lights sweeping the pre-dawn darkness.

It was National Finals Rodeo week in Vegas. I had fifty cowboys and their guests staying at my ranch, their horse trailers circled like covered wagons from a different century. Now they were being rounded up, lined up against the barn in their boxers and bras, bare feet in the desert dirt. Terrell stood by as our dogs ran wild, barking at the chaos.

"Charlie's not coming back anytime soon," I heard an agent tell my half-naked guests.

The agents were thorough, almost ceremonial, in their search. They expected to find bales of cocaine, I learned later. They'd spent two and a half years investigating me, doing controlled buys from my drivers, building their case. And during their search, they had found what I had become: a financial fraudster, a check kiter, an out-of-control guy trying to keep his empire from crumbling.

They took my Rolex watches and about seven grand in cash I had from gambling the night before. Small things, considering what I'd already lost. Standing there in handcuffs, watching them go through my life, I had a strange thought: just twelve hours ago, I'd been in a VIP room at the casino, throwing around money like I'd never run out. Twenty-four hours before that, I'd been worried about which Ferrari to drive to dinner.

Now, I was watching my world end in real time.

By the time they finished, the sun was rising over Las Vegas. The tactical teams were replaced by forensic units, and the violence of the breach gave way to the methodical gathering of evidence. My ranch, which had hosted some of the biggest names in rodeo, now looked like a crime scene because that's exactly what it was.

In the distance, I could see news vans arriving. Local television would have a field day: the limousine king of Las Vegas, brought down by the FBI. The only thing that knocked me off the front page was the Sandy Hook shooting the next day. Sometimes, even infamy gets overshadowed.

The casino called within hours. My cars were banned from their properties. All of them, effective immediately. Even legitimate pickups would be turned away.

The empire I'd built on relationships crumbled in real time, phone call by phone call, cancellation by cancellation.

* * *

But there was one surprise that morning.

A beautiful, twenty-seven-year-old woman named Megan, who had only known me for three months—who had only seen the charming side of Charlie Horky—didn't run.

I was arrested early in the morning and taken downtown for a public arraignment while the FBI went through my house. My sister-in-law, Margot, called Megan and told her what happened.

She immediately got in the car and drove from Novato, California, to my house in Vegas.

I'm sure her father had some pretty choice words for her. At that point, I had absolutely nothing left, but she drove by herself to be with me. While my world collapsed around me, while the agents cataloged the evidence of my crimes, she stayed.

"What do you need?" she asked simply.

I looked at her, this beautiful girl from California, standing in the wreckage of my life. I had no answer. For the first time in decades, I had no move to make, no angle to play, no solution to buy, or scheme to hatch.

The tactical teams took seven hours to complete their search. When they were done, they took me away in handcuffs.

As I rode off in the back of the car to the FBI station in Las Vegas, the special agent said to me, "You must be relieved after all you've been doing."

And he was right. I felt something unexpected: relief. The chase was over. The schemes, the lies, the constant juggling—they were done. I was fifty-two years old, facing twenty years in federal prison, and somehow, I felt lighter than I had in years.

I just didn't know then that this wasn't the end of my story. It was the beginning of a different one.

REDEMPTION
(2012-Present)

After the FBI raid, I had nothing left but a document—THE UNITED STATES OF AMERICA vs. CHARLES JOSEPH HORKY III.

Pretty fucking sobering when you see your name written like that.

I'd gone through $300 million in my career. Now, I couldn't even keep my son's leased car. One by one, everything was collected: almost six million worth of vehicles were repossessed by Titus Leasing. My world unraveled, thread by thread.

The Vegas news stations were having a field day. They talked about life sentences, making my kids terrified I'd die in prison. I was 52. Twenty years felt like a life sentence.

My daughter stopped talking to me. To my great sadness, we haven't spoken since. It could be because I had to extinguish her trust fund when JP Morgan, the bank where the trust was held, refused to maintain the account. The bank wired me the contents of her trust and at the time, I had no choice; I needed it for legal fees.

By that point, I had paid Lauren millions of dollars in divorce settlements. With those payouts, I figured she could help Quinn get through college (she did), if not help me with my legal fees (she absolutely did not).

My lawyer, David Chesnoff, didn't sugar-coat the damage I was facing. "This is a million-dollar case," he said. He might as well have said ten million for all I could afford. "Go find some money, or your ex-wife's going to spend the next fifteen years taking your kids to see you at Christmas time in Lompoc."

Friends stepped up. Tuff Hedeman (rodeo star) brought me $15,000 in cash. My old friend Michael Yamaki met me by the tennis courts at Riviera Country Club—"so they can't record us over the sound of the balls," he said—and gave me back $35,000 of the $200,000 I had paid in membership fees.

The two and a half years between arrest and prison were purgatory. You're not in the news anymore, but nobody wants to do real business with you either. We scraped by with ten cars and some cash hustlers, making maybe $300 a day per car. Survival mode.

Megan continued to be the only bright spot in my life. Her father probably told her I'd be "tied up for quite some time," but, as I mentioned earlier, she had other ideas. She drove to Vegas after my arrest, and she never left.

Out of all the women I'd known, all the rock stars I'd driven, all the success I'd had, nothing showed me what truly mattered in life until I met her. She wasn't wired for the money, the flash. Her parents had been married for forty years. She was just… decent.

When I finally took the plea deal—46 months for racketeering—the judge surprised me. He'd read the thirty letters from people saying I was flawed—but not evil. He understood I was trying to save my company and keep 450 people employed. They'd spent two and a half years investigating me. They had been expecting El Chapo's cousin. Instead, they found a poor bastard who couldn't say no to helping people.

When someone at my company died, I'd pay their widow three years' salary. When someone needed an operation they couldn't afford, I'd cover it. The FBI interviewed everyone: my drivers, even the girls leaving my house at night. Nobody would say a bad word.

Two and a half years after my arrest, on the night before I had to surrender myself to the authorities, Megan drove with me from Vegas to her folks' place in Novato for one last night of freedom. I was ready to go; I just wanted to "self surrender" and get it over with. Megan had lived at my house those two and a half years, but I ended up in prison in Sheridan, Oregon, which was north of her family's home in Novato.

In those grim weeks before I went away, I did have one stroke of luck. I met a lady named Dana Prescott, a newcomer to the limousine business who was just starting out. Even I accepted reality: my life in that business was over. So I made a handshake deal with Dana, and for $180,000, she walked away with my cell phone number.

Overnight, she bought a lifetime of contacts in the business. And I bought Megan the cash flow and security she needed to build the life that, one day, would have me back in it.

That was a lucky break. It looked like I would have some kind of life when I got out. I was grateful that, in some way, I could prepare for my—for our—future together.

Still, nothing prepares you for that moment when you have to walk through those prison doors.

* * *

Prison wasn't what I expected. When you self-surrender, there's all this buildup, this dread of what's waiting for you. But at Sheridan, it was almost anticlimactic. Sign some papers, grab your bedroll, walk back out the same door you came in. They just point you down the street toward the camp and tell you someone will show you to your bunk.

The first thing that hit me was what wasn't there. There was no fence around the property. No towers with armed guards. In twenty-two months, I never saw a naked man or a fistfight. When people talk about "Club Fed," this is what they mean. It was like a men's camp. Just one you couldn't leave.

The prison had different levels: camp, low, medium, high, and apex. I was at the camp level, where they put the white-collar guys and non-violent drug offenders. Anyone with a sentence between one and ten years. We slept in dorms arranged like wings, with a central lobby area full of computer banks for email. Each wing had its own bathroom, and inside, there were eight cubicles with four bunks each, separated by little walls with desks.

Money worked differently inside. If you could spend $600 a month, you were practically a billionaire. I managed to keep myself comfortable—nice clothes, all the necessities—without doing anything that would get me in trouble. Some guys would order food from outside: pizza, McDonald's, Taco Bell. You could even get a cell phone if you wanted.

But all those extras meant risking more time, so I played it straight. I worked the inside angles instead.

After about six months, I started figuring out how things really worked—who did what, who could make things happen, who to avoid. I got along with everybody: the Islanders, the Blacks, the Whites, the Mexicans. My years in the transportation business had taught me how to read people, how to find common ground.

The residential drug and alcohol program—RDAP, they called it—was the real education at Sheridan. Nine months of group therapy, stuck in rooms with guys sharing stories that ranged from tragic to absurd. Some of these men had lost everything: families, fortunes, decades of their lives to addiction. Every time I thought I'd hit bottom, someone would share a story that made my problems seem almost manageable. I sat through story after story of people who thought they were too smart, too successful, too something to end up where they ended up.

Some of it felt like going through the motions. Playing cornhole in the yard, doing trust falls, therapeutic bullshit. But something was working loose in me. Maybe it was hearing my own story reflected back through all these different lives. Maybe it was finally having nowhere to run, no problem I could solve by throwing money at it.

The program was also a ticket to freedom. Complete it successfully, and they'd take a year off your sentence. Add that to the good time credit—14.5% of your sentence—and another six months off for early release because of the program, and my 46-month sentence dropped to 22 months. Plenty of guys tried to game the system, saying whatever they thought the counselors wanted to hear. But after a while, I started to realize that maybe the point wasn't getting out early. Maybe it was about understanding why I'd ended up there in the first place.

All through my stay, Megan was my lifeline to the outside world. Every four or five weeks, she'd make the trek to Sheridan, Oregon, stay in some dump of a motel, and spend two full days with me. Playing cards, eating terrible food, planning our future.

When you're inside, those visits are everything. They're proof that someone out there still cares—still believes in you.

My kids didn't come to see me. Neither did my mom. Not because they didn't want to; it would have just been too hard. I didn't need them to put themselves through that. But I was grateful for every time Megan and our son together, Andrew, came to see me. Her father even came to see me near the end of my time. He asked what my plans were when I got out.

"I'm going to marry your daughter," I told him.

He seemed happy about that. "When you get back," he said, "it's not going to be like it was before, but she's tried awfully hard to make it as nice as it can be."

My physical transformation, too, was dramatic. I went in weighing 240 pounds, all that excess from years of Vegas living. Through the prison routine and maybe just the stripping away of all the stress of maintaining my old life, I got down to 177. I was in the best shape I'd been in for decades. I learned about myself, about addiction, about the difference between success and worth.

Inside, you have a lot of time to think. About where you went wrong, about what really matters. I started reimagining what my business could be. I realized I didn't need to own cars anymore.

Cars had been my ticket to riches, but they had also been my downfall, trying to maintain this massive fleet while the economy was crumbling.

Although, frankly, I couldn't have started back up in that work even if I wanted to. When I finally got out and found myself on a Southwest flight back to Vegas, I thought, *what now?* I headed to a halfway house, and I felt like life had reset itself to 1980. I didn't even have enough money for a car.

* * *

I needed a job, and thankfully, a friend named Mike Haggerty gave me one selling buses for $72,000 a year. For someone who used to make millions, that $6,000 a month felt like peanuts. But it was a lifeline, and I was grateful for it.

Then everything changed again with one phone call.

Bobby Baldwin, the former president of City Center and a legend in Vegas, called me in. "Kid," he said, looking at me across his desk at ARIA, "I don't think the streets are paved with gold anymore in this town. It's different with Uber. You can't get a license personally anymore. What are you going to do?"

I explained a few ideas that I had started developing in prison, and he disappeared into his back room. He came back with what looked like a shoe bag. Inside was $50,000 in cash. In the old days—my old life—that would have been pocket change. But now, that $50,000 was rocket fuel.

It gave me the capital to launch SLADE: Special Logistics and Delivery Experts. The business model was completely different from my old companies. Instead of owning cars, we'd be a reservation management company. Take Nicki Minaj, my first client. She might need four cars to pick her up at JFK and take her to her hotel. Each car would cost about $400, so I needed $1,600 in capital because no limo company would extend credit to an ex-felon convicted of financial crimes. But with Bobby's money, I could front these costs.

The key was changing how we handled payments. Back in the nineties, asking a client for a credit card was practically an insult. Everyone got billed and paid whenever they felt like it. Now, every account had to be secured by a credit card upfront. No exceptions. I hate chasing money. As far as I'm concerned, it's not my job to finance people's ground transportation—that's what their credit cards are for. I've had that policy for the past seven years, and it's served me well. By 2017, people understood that it was just standard business practice.

What amazed me was how the old clients started coming back. Mick Jagger, Sting, different people who'd been with me for decades. But Sting was special. He was the only one who hadn't abandoned me when I was going to prison.

When his Rainforest Foundation was planning their final concert at The Beacon Theatre in New York City, its 30th Anniversary Benefit Concert titled "We'll Be Together"—this huge event with James Taylor and all these celebrities performing—I went to him and Billy, his tour manager. I asked to handle the transportation. It was a massive job, about $40,000 worth of work. Fresh out of prison, that was a huge risk for me. But I did the whole thing for free and sent them a bill marked "no charge." Not for business—for loyalty.

Six months later, I saw Sting in San Francisco during his play, "The Last Ship." Just the way he looked at me, I knew he understood what I'd done. It wasn't long before I was given his tour all over the United States. He basically put me back on the map.

Sting and me at the airport (LAX, 1985).

The business grew faster than I could have imagined. Word spread. Christian Ortiz, who handled Mick Jagger's personal affairs, brought the Rolling Stones tour to me. Shawn Gee and Gee Roberson, major managers in the music industry, connected me with Amir Thompson, aka Questlove. The dominoes started falling.

In just the last five months of my first year back, SLADE did $576,000. The next year, we hit $2.5 million, then $3.5 million.

The best part?

No overhead.

No car payments, no insurance, no employees to manage. Just relationships and service—the parts I'd always been good at.

The industry started believing in me again because I was becoming a power player, just differently this time. When I paid contractors, they got paid on time. My age, experience, and history—frankly, even the fall of CLS—gave me a kind of credibility. They started calling me "the legend" at industry conventions, asking me to speak about everything I've learned.

Every day, I sit in my office surrounded by gold records from Guns N' Roses, Depeche Mode, U2, Quincy Jones, Michael Jackson, and Elton John. They're not just decorations—they're reminders. Reminders of where I've been, what I've lost, and what really matters. This time around, I'm not trying to be the biggest. I'm just trying to be the best at what I do—zero tolerance for failure.

The money's good—better than I expected. But it's different now. It's not about private jets and Ferraris. It's about building something sustainable, something I can be proud of. Something that honors the trust people like Sting and Bobby Baldwin placed in me when everyone else had written me off.

* * *

And of course, there was Megan, who stuck with me through the arrest, through the pre-sentencing limbo, and through prison. When I got out, we got married, just as I had promised her father.

Megan is still standing by me (Aspen, Colorado).

In 2018, we bought a house in a guard-gated community. It's where I currently live with Megan and Andrew. We have four dogs, three cats, fifteen chickens, and a horse. I know all my neighbors.

It's not all a fairytale ending. To my regret, I have no relationship with my daughter. She graduated from UCLA Law School without me there. She can't see any use for me in her life, and I have to respect her choice.

But my son and I are thick as thieves. I get to know him as a person now, not just as the son of a man with private jets and multiple homes.

Me and my son Hunter (in the early days).

My industry colleagues, who now view me as a legend and a fountain of wisdom, often ask me for advice.

But I can offer a warning: success without foundation is just failure in disguise.

I'm sixty-four years old now. Every day, I wake up in a home where I'm loved. I support my mother, who's turning eighty-eight this year. I'm a contributing member of society. I've seen hundreds of millions pass through my fingers, lost it all, and found something worth more.

They say my story would make a good movie. Maybe it would.

But I hope it makes a better lesson: It's never too late to change.

And sometimes, the biggest gift is losing everything that doesn't matter.

THANK YOU FOR READING MY BOOK!

DOWNLOAD YOUR FREE GIFTS

Just to say thanks for buying and reading my book,
I would like to connect with you!

Scan the QR Code:

I appreciate your interest in my book, and value your feedback as it helps me improve future versions of this book. I would appreciate it if you could leave your invaluable review on Amazon.com with your feedback. Thank you!

www.ingramcontent.com/pod-product-compliance
Lightning Source LLC
LaVergne TN
LVHW011425080426
835512LV00005B/272